EPIC

EPIC BOOKS are no ordinary books. They burst with intense action, high-speed heroics, and shadows of the unknown. Are you ready for an Epic adventure?

This edition first published in 2024 by Bellwether Media, Inc.

No part of this publication may be reproduced in whole or in part without written permission of the publisher. For information regarding permission, write to Bellwether Media, Inc., Attention: Permissions Department, 6012 Blue Circle Drive, Minnetonka, MN 55343.

Library of Congress Cataloging-in-Publication Data

Names: Sabelko, Rebecca, author.
Title: Amargasaurus / by Rebecca Sabelko.
Description: Minneapolis, MN : Bellwether Media, 2024. | Series: The world of dinosaurs | Includes bibliographical references and index. | Audience: Ages 7-12 | Audience: Grades 4-6 | Summary: "Engaging images accompany information about the amargasaurus. The combination of high-interest subject matter and light text is intended for students in grades 2 through 7"-- Provided by publisher.
Identifiers: LCCN 2023020267 (print) | LCCN 2023020268 (ebook) | ISBN 9798886875027 (library binding) | ISBN 9798886875522 (paperback) | ISBN 9798886876901 (ebook)
Subjects: LCSH: Amargasaurus--Juvenile literature. | Dinosaurs--Juvenile literature.
Classification: LCC QE862.S3 S23224 2024 (print) | LCC QE862.S3 (ebook) | DDC 567.913--dc23/eng/20230506
LC record available at https://lccn.loc.gov/2023020267
LC ebook record available at https://lccn.loc.gov/2023020268

Text copyright © 2024 by Bellwether Media, Inc. EPIC and associated logos are trademarks and/or registered trademarks of Bellwether Media, Inc.

Editor: Rachael Barnes   Designer: Jeffrey Kollock

Printed in the United States of America, North Mankato, MN.

TABLE OF CONTENTS

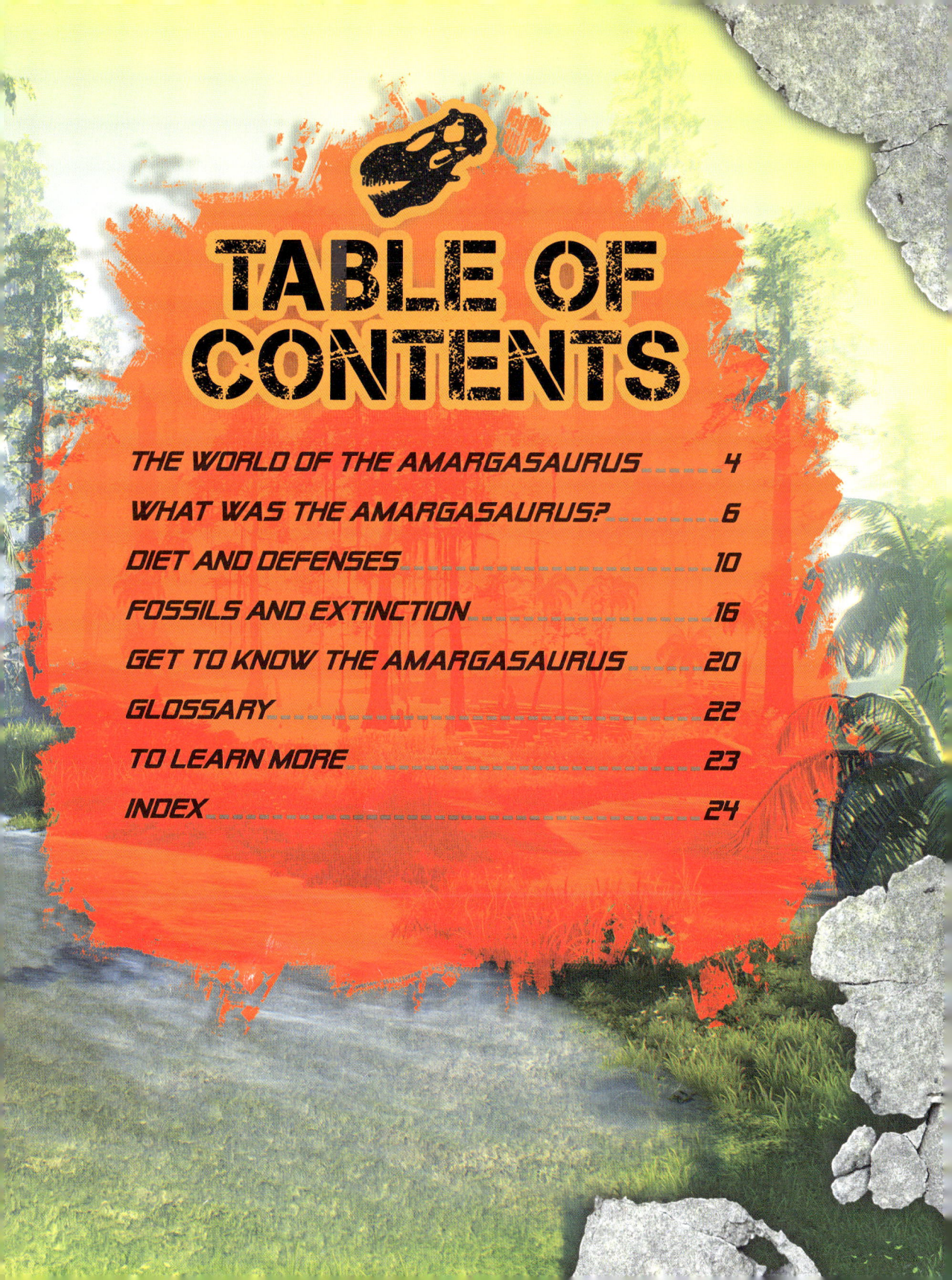

THE WORLD OF THE AMARGASAURUS 4
WHAT WAS THE AMARGASAURUS? 6
DIET AND DEFENSES 10
FOSSILS AND EXTINCTION 16
GET TO KNOW THE AMARGASAURUS 20
GLOSSARY 22
TO LEARN MORE 23
INDEX 24

THE WORLD OF THE AMARGASAURUS

sail

The amargasaurus was a **sauropod**. It likely had two **sails** on its neck! It lived around 130 million years ago. This was during the Early **Cretaceous period** of the **Mesozoic era**.

MAP OF THE WORLD

Early Cretaceous period

NAME GAME

The amargasaurus is named after an area of land called La Amarga. It is in Argentina. This is where the dinosaur's fossils were discovered!

PRONUNCIATION

ah-MAR-guh-SORE-us

WHAT WAS THE AMARGASAURUS?

Some sauropods grew over 100 feet (30 meters) long. But the amargasaurus was much smaller.

It reached up to 43 feet (13 meters) long.
It weighed over 8,000 pounds (3,629 kilograms).

TROUBLE SMELLING

Many scientists believe the amargasaurus could not smell well. The part of its brain that controlled its sense of smell was very small.

SIZE CHART

25 feet (8 meters)
15 feet (5 meters)
5 feet (2 meters)

spines

This dinosaur had long **spines** on its neck and back. Skin likely covered the neck spines to form sails. The amargasaurus may have used them to show off to other dinosaurs.

Three curved claws on its back feet helped it dig nests.

LONG SPINES

The amargasaurus's longest spines were on the middle of its neck. They reached 24 inches (61 centimeters) long!

nest

DIET AND DEFENSES

The amargasaurus had a shorter neck than other sauropods. It could not lift its head high.

It likely ate tough ground plants.
It may have eaten leaves from low trees.

AMARGASAURUS DIET

leafy plants

ferns

tree leaves

11

It pulled leaves off plants with its long teeth. It swallowed food whole.

It may have swallowed stones. The stones helped the dinosaur break down its food.

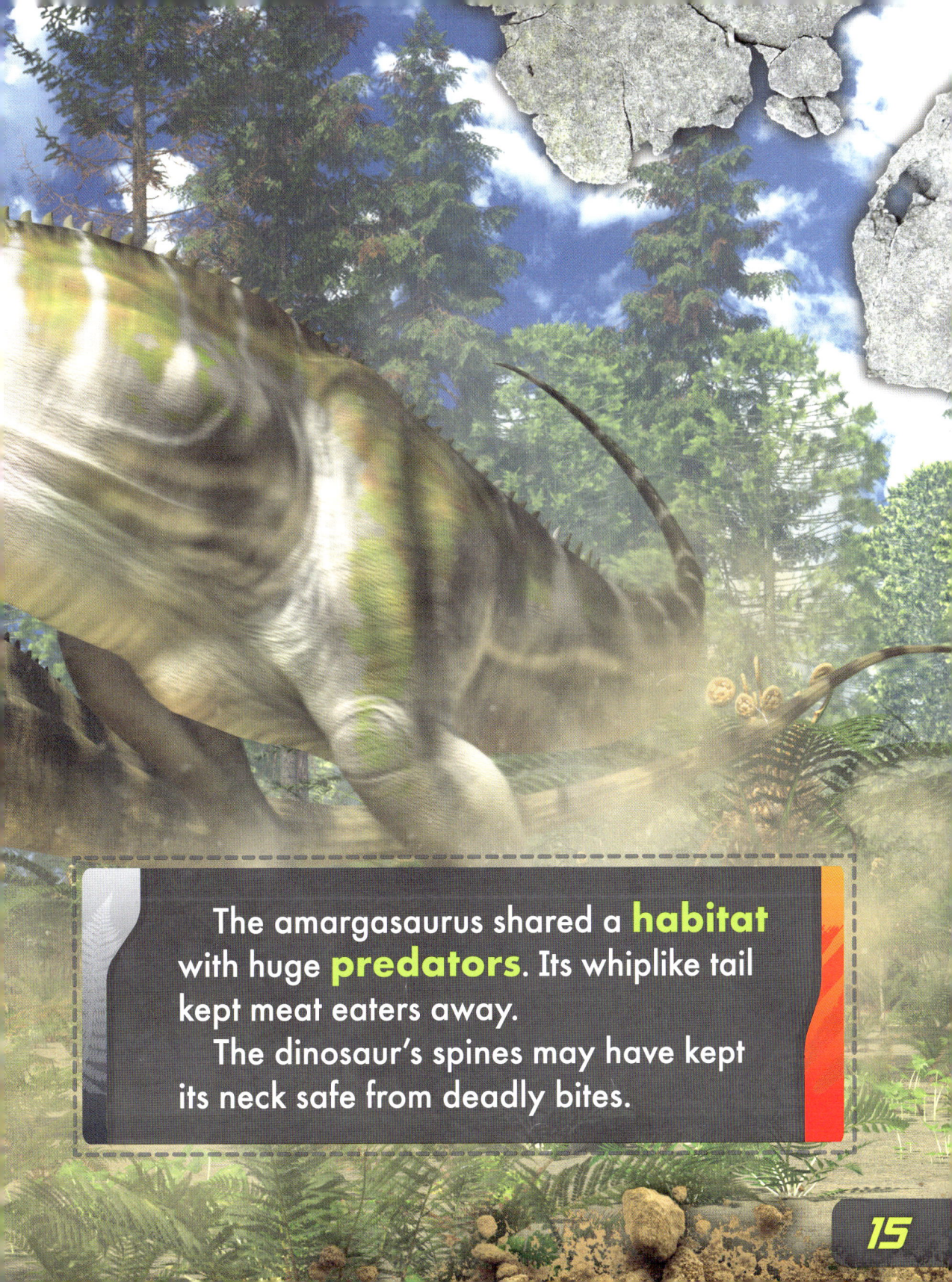

The amargasaurus shared a **habitat** with huge **predators**. Its whiplike tail kept meat eaters away.

The dinosaur's spines may have kept its neck safe from deadly bites.

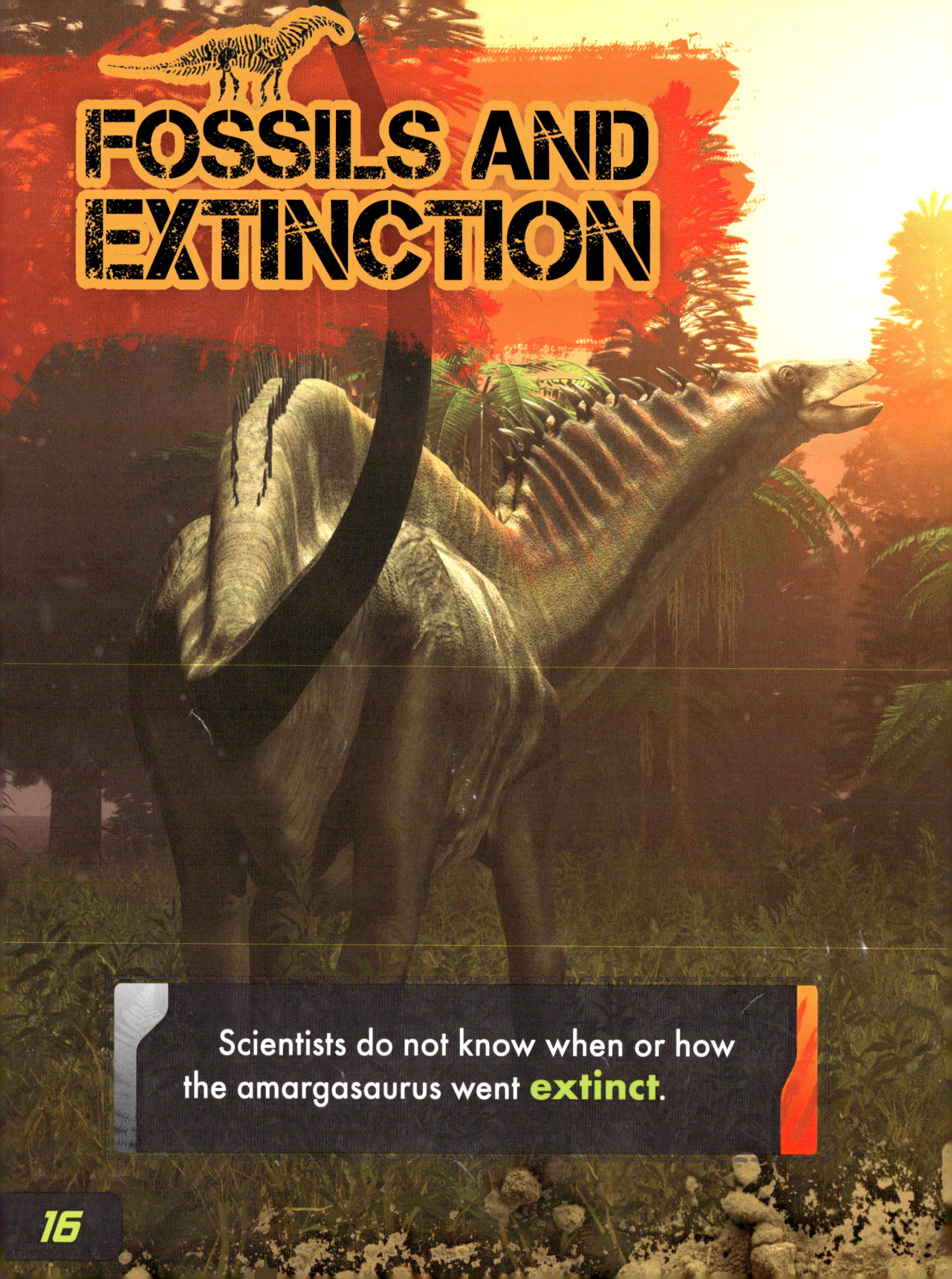

FOSSILS AND EXTINCTION

Scientists do not know when or how the amargasaurus went **extinct**.

Earth went through many changes throughout the Cretaceous period. These changes may have made life hard for the dinosaur.

Amargasaurus **fossils** were found in Argentina in 1984.

amargasaurus fossil

GET TO KNOW THE AMARGASAURUS

⚠ FIRST FOSSILS FOUND
La Amarga Formation, Argentina, in 1984

spines

sail

HEIGHT up to 12 feet (3.7 meters) tall at the shoulder

⚠ FOUND BY
Guillermo Rougier

LENGTH up to 43 feet (13 meters) long

20

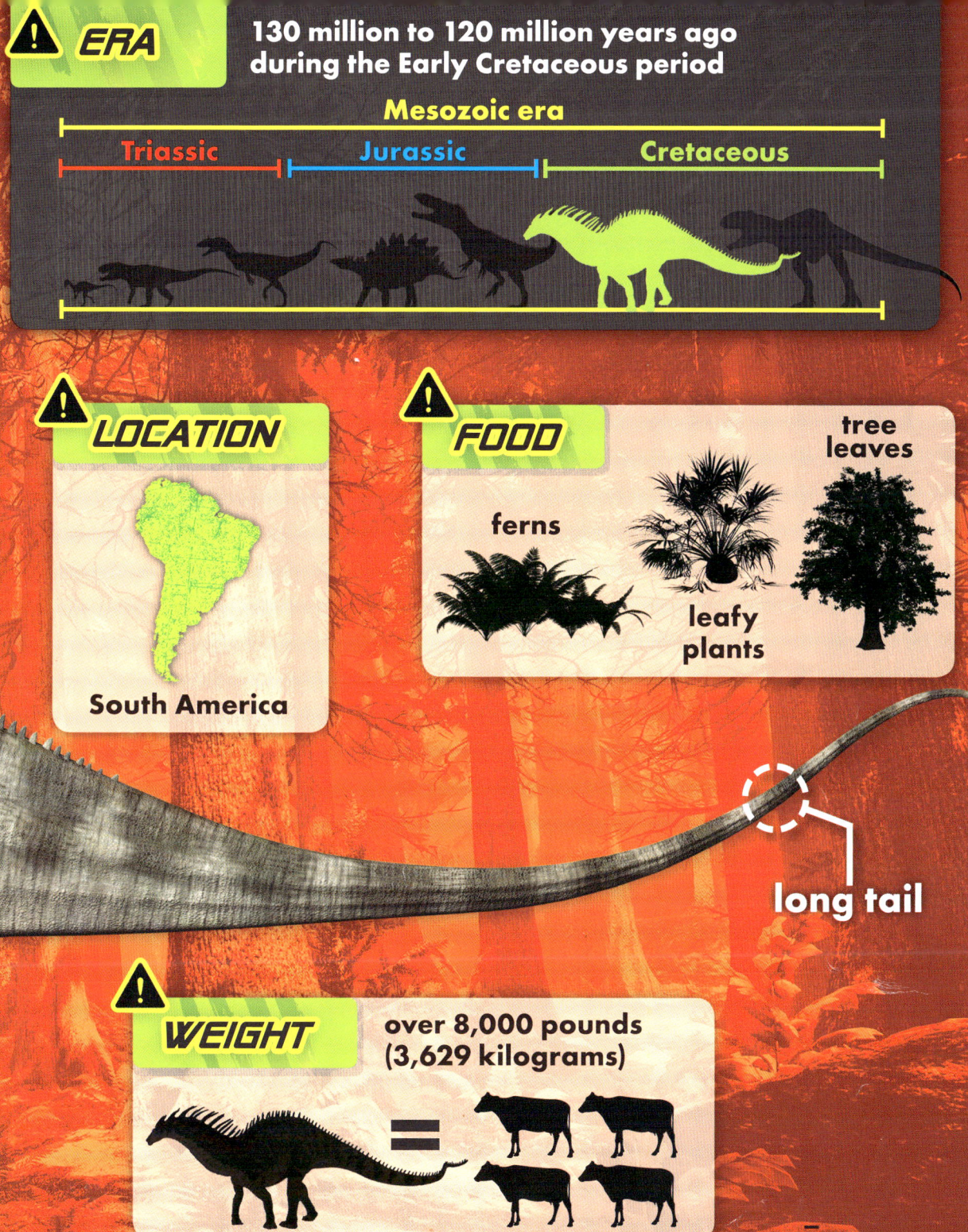

GLOSSARY

Cretaceous period—the last period of the Mesozoic era that occurred between 145 million and 66 million years ago; the Early Cretaceous period began around 145 million years ago.

extinct—no longer living

fossils—the remains of living things that lived long ago

habitat—a home or area where animals prefer to live

Mesozoic era—a time in history in which dinosaurs lived on Earth; the first birds, mammals, and flowering plants appeared on Earth during the Mesozoic era.

predators—animals that hunt other animals for food

sails—long spines connected by skin that grew out of the neck and back of the amargasaurus

sauropod—a four-legged dinosaur that ate plants and lived during the Jurassic and Cretaceous periods; sauropods had small heads and long necks and tails.

spines—long bones connected to a dinosaur's backbones

TO LEARN MORE

AT THE LIBRARY

Braun, Eric. *Could You Survive the Cretaceous Period?: An Interactive Prehistoric Adventure*. North Mankato, Minn.: Capstone Press, 2020.

Hibbert, Clare. *Giant Dinosaurs: Sauropods*. New York, N.Y.: Enslow Publishing, 2018.

Sabelko, Rebecca. *Argentinosaurus*. Minneapolis, Minn.: Bellwether Media, 2021.

ON THE WEB

FACTSURFER

Factsurfer.com gives you a safe, fun way to find more information.

1. Go to www.factsurfer.com.

2. Enter "amargasaurus" into the search box and click 🔍.

3. Select your book cover to see a list of related web sites.

INDEX

Argentina, 5, 18
back, 8
claws, 9
Early Cretaceous period, 4, 5, 17
extinct, 16
food, 11, 12, 13
fossils, 5, 18, 19
get to know, 20–21
habitat, 15
head, 10
map, 5, 19
Mesozoic era, 4
name, 5

neck, 4, 8, 9, 10, 15
nests, 9
predators, 15
pronunciation, 5
sails, 4, 8
sauropod, 4, 6, 10
scientists, 7, 16, 19
size, 6, 7, 9, 10, 12
smell, 7
spines, 8, 9, 15
stones, 13
tail, 15
teeth, 12

The images in this book are reproduced through the courtesy of: James Kuether, front cover, pp. 4-5, 6-7, 8-9, 10-11, 11 (all plants), 12-13, 14-15, 16-17, 20-21; william cushman, pp. 18-19.